1

Carol Ann Duffy is Poet Laureate and Professor of
Contemporary Poetry at Manchester Metropolitan
University, where she is also Creative Director of the
Writing School. Her poetry for both children and adults
has received many awards, most recently the Costa
Poetry Award for *The Bees* (2011). She was awarded the
PEN Pinter Prize in 2012 and *Ritual Lighting* (*Laureate
Poems*) was published in 2014. Her other work for theatre,
published by Faber, includes *Grimm Tales*, *Beasts and
Beauties* and *Rats' Tales*.

also by Carol Ann Duffy for Faber Drama

CAROL ANN DUFFY

Everyman

a new adaptation

FABER & FABER

First published in 2015
by Faber and Faber Limited
74–77 Great Russell Street
London WC1B 3DA

This edition with final amendments June 2015

Typeset by Country Setting, Kingsdown, Kent CT14 8ES
Printed in England by CPI Group (UK) Ltd, Croydon CR0 4YY

A CIP record for this book is available from the British Library

ISBN 978-0-571-32688-4

For Rufus Norris
with love

Everyman in this adaptation was first produced in the Olivier auditorium of the National Theatre, London, on 29 April 2015. The cast was as follows:

Everyman Chiwetel Ejiofor
God / Good Deeds Kate Duchêne
Death Dermot Crowley

FELLOWSHIP/SENSES & WITS

Paul Bullion (**Sound**)
Adam Burton (**Passion**)
Amy Griffiths (**Vanity**)
Nick Holder (**Strength**)
Nicholas Karimi (**Smell**)
Joshua Lacey (**Sensuality**)
Ira Mandela Siobhan (**Sight**)
Coral Messam (**Conscience**)
Amanda Minihan (**Touch**)
Itxaso Moreno (**Taste**)
Kiruna Stamell (**Discretion**)
Clemmie Sveaas (**Insecurity**)

KINDRED

Sharon D. Clarke (**Mother**)
Philip Martin Brown (**Father**)
Michelle Butterly (**Sister**)

GOODS

Adam Burton, Amy Griffiths, Joshua Lacey,
Clemmie Sveaas

Knowledge Penny Layden
Everyboy Jeshaiah Murray / Tumo Reetsang /
   Joshua Tikare
Ensemble Stephen Aintree

Director Rufus Norris
*Choreographer and Movement Direct*or Javier De Frutos
Set Designer Ian MacNeil
Costume Designer Nicky Gillibrand
Lighting Designer Paul Anderson
Video Designer Tal Rosner
Music William Lyons
Sound Designer Paul Arditti
Music Production Dominic Betmead
Vocal Music Director Stephen Higgins
Company Voice Work Kate Godfrey
Staff Director Emily Lim
Stage Manager Laura Flowers
Deputy Stage Manager Jo Nield
Assistant Stage Managers Stuart Campbell,
   Tom Gilding

A special thanks from Carol Ann Duffy to Emily Lim,
Jo Nield and Laura Flowers.

EVERYMAN

God/Good Deeds (*finishes cleaning stage*)
Good day at work?
                        You find me at my work –
She who cleans the room before the party,
Mops up afterwards . . . a vicious circle . . .
Skivvying for those who are immortal.
Or so they think. I see you have your drink.
Prosecco? Seize the moment while it lasts! While it lasts.
                    All done. Shipshape and Bristol fashion;
Ready for the dancing, boozing, passion –
Oh yes, I'll be sweeping condoms up
Before this night is done – and worse. Don't ask.
I'm nothing if not thorough, caring, dutiful.
And you . . . are all so beautiful.

Prologue: Everyman's birthday party with Fellowship,
which descends into drunkenness, coke-snorting, lewdness
and aggression amidst the dancing and laughter. The
prologue ends with a rap and Everyman vomiting into
a bucket provided by God/Good Deeds.

Fellowship (*rapping*)
Masters of the Universe
listen to my rap verse
Masters of the Universe
listen to my rap verse
Masters of the Universe

24/7 livin in Heaven, revvin up the lifestyle, bevvies
    with the brethren,

3

Tinker tailor soldier I spy, camel don't pass thru a
    needle's eye,
Rich man, poor man, beggarman, thief, beyond
    redemption, beyond belief,
Happy fuckin birthday, woof woof, hair of the dog,
Masters of the Universe, you're –
listen to me listen to me – you're God.
What's God like God like God like God like –
you're God-like, listen to the truth.

24/7 gotta make a livin, on my second wife –
    I, upgradin on the Wifi,
revvin up the revvin up the revvin up the lifestyle,
Rich as Croesus, thank you Jesus, connected to the
    thigh-bone
is the fuckin iPhone,
Happy fuckin birthday, woof woof, beware of the dog,
Masters of the Universe you're –
listen to me listen to me – you're God.
What's God like God like God like God like –
you're God-like – listen to the truth.

Everyman vomits.

Everyman
    Oh my God . . .

God/Good Deeds
    What's God like? Hear my voice –
    though I've been their shepherd, of their world the light,
    have walked on water, raised the dead, self-resurrected,
    so it's been said, turned water into wine . . .
    or, verily, I was when nothing was
    and I will be when nothing else remains;
    sent several prophets to explain all this,
    have clicked on like a pilot-light above apostles' heads,
    and what they think I think is to be found
    in all their Holy Tomes – Torah, Bible, Koran –
        or scriptures –

4

that which is heard, that which is remembered –
despite all this, my prayer remains unanswered.
For I perceive here in my majesty
how all mankind grows worse from year to year,
cavorting with Wrath, Greed, Sloth,
with Pride, Lust, Envy and with Gluttony.
It seems that Everyman has had enough of me
or takes my name in vain. The angels weep
to see the ruin of the Earth:
the gathered waters, which I called the seas,
unclean, choking on themselves.
The dry land – fractured, fracked.
The firmament so full of filth,
my two Great Lights, to rule the day and night,
have tears in their eyes.
                          I gave the tree, yielding fruit,
whose seed is in itself; abundant fish,
great singing whales, winged fowl, cattle,
every living beast I could imagine. Behold, it was
   all good,
all good. And now? All trashed. For why?
For Everyman liveth only for his pleasure.
Therefore, I will have Reckoning with Everyman.
Amen to that. I hoped well once that he
would make his mansion in my glory
and so I made him hero of the story,
the lazy, selfish, thoughtless, thankless fool.
But, should I show myself, he'd not believe.
I need a mighty messenger. Where art thou, Death?

Death
Almighty, Governor, I'm here, at your command,
awaiting orders. Suited, booted, scythe in hand.

God/Good Deeds
Death – trump card, final word – pay Everyman a call
and show him, in my omnipresent name,

5

the final journey he must undertake,
right now, and can't escape. Impress upon him
he must bring a Reckoning to me
of how he's used the time I've granted him.
You get my drift? *Comprendez? Samjha?*
My will is set on this.

Death

Thy Will Be Done. I'll find an Everyman
most typical of one who's squandered his God-given
    time
on pleasure, treasure, leisure, etcetera. The world
    is full of them
and my dead eyes see all the world at once.

Everyman groans.

Sorted.

*Everyman gives God/Good Deeds £10 for clearing his
vomit.*

Everyman

Bless you.

Death

Here's one arriving now
with no thought in his hedonistic head
that Death will, pronto, buttonhole him in his tracks.

Enter Everyman on to balcony.

Amazing view.

Everyman

I'm seeing two of it. Birthday bash.
I need a slash.

Death

That's right.
Piss on the world, as usual.

Everyman
Look, mate, don't go starting anything . . .

Death
How's your soul?

Everyman
What?

Death
Have you forgotten God?

Everyman
Oh my days.

Death
Omnipotent? All-seeing?
A word in your shell-like.
God's been watching you.
You're on God's mind.

Everyman
I think you're confusing me with someone else.

Death
Your card is marked. I know your name, son.
The hour is later than you think
and I've been sent to you by God. Specifically.

Everyman
God? By God?
Get out of my face.

Death
Not possible. Not an option. No way out.
It's in your interests not to doubt
God has a plan for you. Everyman.

Everyman
Who told you my name?
I have nothing to do with any creed –

live and let live, that's my philosophy.
Go and peck at someone else's swede.

Death

Read my lips.
My Governor wants a Reckoning. Of your life.
No ifs or buts, no bottling it, no *mañana*. Man-up time.
Here's the itinerary.
You leave here now and make a pilgrimage to God.
Then you explain yourself.

Everyman

Yeah, yeah, yeah.

Everyman reels back as Death grasps him.

Your touch is ice.

Death

The moment's now.
The journey long, hard, dangerous.
You can't decline.
Start counting up your many bad deeds
and those puny few, your good.
You'll tell the score to God. In 'Paradise'.
Carpe diem don't apply.
There you'll be judged
on how you've spent your temporary life.
Yes, rack your brain for one good deed.
There won't be anyone to intercede.

Everyman

Who are you?

Death

I'm Death. God's Heavy, if you like.
Yes, you know me now all right.
I always see it in the eyes.

Everyman

Leave me alone.

Death

My calling-card: cancer, famine, war, a virus
or a plague, great fires and floods. You know the score.

Everyman

This is sick.

Death

Sic transit gloria mundi, my old son.
Your time on Earth is done.

Everyman

I'm in my fucking prime!

Death

I spare no living man. Why act as though
you are immortal and I'll never show?

Everyman

Let me go.

Death

No.

Everyman

Not here, like this.
I swear to you,
I'll pay whatever you ask.
I'm loaded! I'm successful!
Name your price.

Death

That won't be happening.
I can't be bought with gold and silver,
readies, dosh, spondulicks, plastic, notes.
Nor by politicians, princes, priests or popes,
or poets, painters, pimps. No drug baron or oligarch
can grease this palm. Start reckoning.

Everyman

Help! Somebody help me!

I've had no warning from you.
I don't have any Reckoning worth mentioning.
More years! Give me more years!
I'm begging you!

Death

Get up. Don't blubber like a big girl's blouse.
Stop grovelling. It's not a pretty sight. Wipe that snot.
You'll start this journey now and do what's right.
No man cheats Death. I'm always up ahead.
Each one of you will know that when you're dead.

Everyman

This is a headfuck.
Please please please . . .
I have good friends. I have a family.
This will destroy them.

Death

Destroy them? There's an idea.
Oh! You want to take them with you?
Heavens to Murgatroyd –
It's worth a try.

Everyman

I only have one life!
It's not my time!

Death

Only on loan, my son, only on loan.
And once you've gone, there'll be another one along
who'll get it wrong. A waste of space
who does not see me eyeballing his face.
What's my name?

Everyman

Death. I see you.
I see the end of days, of mornings, nights . . .
then endless sorrow.
Can't we make a deal – sort this tomorrow?

Death

No can do. It doesn't work like that. I make white
    black,
zap, embolism, stroke, or car crash, heart attack.
I'm hard. Your life's a candle to me. Pff. Snuffed it.
Remember, God created me to sort you out.
Yes, back away – you won't get far!
Oops! Here's the craic –
this beginning is the end.
But you're the sort who'll try to phone a friend.
Good luck with that. Au revoir.

*Everyman slips and falls off the balcony. The rest of
the action takes place in his head during his fall to his
death.*

Death stalks him.

Fellowship

Happy fucking birthday!
Happy fucking birthday!
Happy fucking birthday!
Happy fucking birthday!

Everyman

Guys?

Fellowship

Hooray!

Everyman

Please . . .

Fellowship

Brother from another mother,
give me some love.
What's wrong?
You look like you've seen a ghost.

Get him a shot.
Sit down.

Everyman
Think of your worst nightmare, then treble it.
I'm telling you, I'm in deep shit.

Fellowship
Whoo!

Sings from 'All About That Bass' by Meghan Trainor.

Everyman
Something unbelievable just happened.
Out there on the deck.
I'm fucking spooked.

Fellowship
Here we go.
The wind-up merchant . . .

Get that down you.

Everyman
I'm deadly serious.
Swear to me, no matter what I say,
however weird it sounds, how mad,
how off its head,
you won't abandon me.

Fellowship
Never.

Everyman
No?

Fellowship
All for one
and one for all!

Everyman
Have you ever thought about being dead?

Fellowship
    Every morning with a hangover.

Everyman
    We don't know when it'll happen.
    We just don't know.

Fellowship
    Ev – what's going on?
    Are you OK?

Everyman
    Sinead – I need you. I need you.

Fellowship
    Oooh!

Everyman
    I need you to come with me – now.

Fellowship
    But we're just getting going!

Everyman
    I have to go away; begin a journey –
    what did he say?
    Hard and long and dangerous . . .
    then stand in front – I can hardly get this out –
    then stand in front of God
    and give a fucking Reckoning of my life.

Fellowship
    A Fucking Reckoning will take a while!
    Form an orderly queue . . .

Everyman
    It's insane . . .
    but if I can find some way
    of pitching myself to God –
    with the help of the best mates in the world –
    I might get a reprieve.

What am I saying?
I don't even know if I believe.

You've got to help me.
I can't think straight.

Fellowship

Whoa. Mate. This is seriously off-piste.
You say this journey's hard and long?
And dangerous?
Where's the sodding *joie de vivre* in that?
We love you to bits. You're immense.
But you're not making any sense.

Everyman

And I love you.
And never more than now.

Fellowship

Get here. You're trembling!
Presenting your accounts to God? Total shite.
Is God working for the Inland Revenue now?
Who's filled your head with all this crap?

Everyman

It was Death.

Fellowship

Death?

Everyman

He got me on the balcony.
I smelled his fetid awful breath.
I have to go!

Fellowship

Death wasn't invited here.
If Death shows up, sorry, but we're off.

Everyman

I'm thinking you can big me up!

I'm not a bad person, am I?
I'm considerate.
I can be generous –
I lent you the deposit for your flat.
That might count, yeah?
And we had three great years, Sinead –

Fellowship
Before you screwed it up.

Everyman
I made you happy once –
you could tell God that.

Fellowship
I tell God you were good in bed?

Everyman
I'm a good skin.
I might be a bit fucking flawed,
but I don't deserve this shit.

Fellowship
Ev, chillax. We're still your crew.
Let's pop some corks, open your gifts,
have a sniff, a snort.

Everyman
If you love me . . .

Fellowship
WE DO!

Sings lines from 'You'll Never Walk Alone' by Rodgers and Hammerstein.

Everyman
Just prove it's true!
Come with me. Help me.

Fellowship
But, darling, if we do come with you,
how and when would we get back?

Everyman
I don't know!

Fellowship
This is heavy.
Scary stuff.
I've had enough.
I have to leave. Rather suddenly.
You're having a bad one,
let's wind these celebrations up.

Everyman
You might not see me again!

Fellowship
Everyman, you've been my lover –
till you looked elsewhere . . .
Ditto . . . Ditto . . . Ditto . . .
and you're still one of my dearest friends.
We're your fandom.
But we can't just leave a birthday party
and go to the Afterlife!
It's too random.
We came here to eat, drink, be merry!
You're spoiling your own party!
All this talk of Death . . . and God?
Fucking odd.

Everyman
Where are you going?
What about . . . Fellowship?

Fellowship
We're well out of our comfort zone here.

Everyman
Won't even one of you come with me?
Please?

Fellowship
Ev, I feel your pain, believe me,
and you can have the shirt from off my back,
but this is mental! We have our lives to live.
We can't come with you on this crazy trip.
If it was one of us, you'd say the same.
There's no one here to blame.
Let me hold you. There. Go well.

Fellowship leaves.

Everyman
Bear-hug. Thumbs-up. Then go to Hell.
I might as well have asked the Man in the Moon
to climb down from the sky and walk with me.
Friends? You broke my heart!
Who's there? Who's following me?
Leave me alone!

Everyman runs.

Regroup. Regroup. Think. Think.
Blood is thicker than water –
my family love me.
My mother would do anything for me.
OK. OK. You can sort this.
Keep it together.
Best son. Best son.

Everyman goes to Kindred.

Father
That's our door knocking.
That's a knock at our door.

Sister

Calm down. I'll get it.
It's Ev.

Mother

Everyman! My baby!
What a lovely surprise!
I can't believe my eyes.

Everyman

Give me a hug, Mother.

Mother

Come in, stranger.

Sister

What's this, soft lad? The return of the Prodigal?

Mother

He'll have me in tears.
He's not been home on his birthday for years.

Father

Whose birthday?

Everyman

Hello, Father, it's me.

Father

There was a knock at our door.

Sister

I answered it, Dad.
It's your son, Everyman, isn't it?

Everyman

Hello, Father.

Mother

Home for his birthday.
Home is where the heart is.
I am. I'm filling up.

18

Don't get me started.
Let's celebrate. Open some bubbly.

Sister

Bubbly? There's some Tia Maria left over from your
    Ruby Wedding.
So what's brought this on?
We thought you'd forgotten where we lived.

Father

Someone knows where we live.
They knocked on our door.

Sister

Don't upset yourself, Father.
You should have given us more warning.

Mother

Every time we phone, you're in a meeting.
Have you eaten?
(Get into the fridge for the leftovers.)

Sister

He knows where the kitchen is.

Father

If you can force your heart and nerve and –

Sister

Sinew.

Father

Sinew.
To serve their turn long after they are gone
And so hold on when there is nothing in you
Except the will that says to them –

Mother

Hold on.

Father

Hold on.

Sister

It's all he remembers now. His quotations.

Everyman

Nothing's changed. It's still the same.
Same furniture. That vase.
What's that?

Sister

Well, it's not a fucking Dyson.

Mother

Hush your mouth!

Everyman

What is it?

Father

Whose birthday?

Sister

Mother has to have oxygen.

Mother

I'm fine. Fine.

Everyman

You should have told me . . .

Sister

I did.

Father

Whose birthday?

Everyman

It doesn't matter, Father.
It's only me.
Best son. Best son.
I know I haven't been the world's best son
or brother – but I need you.
You're my flesh and blood.

Sister

    You're coming on a bit strong.

    What's wrong?

Everyman

    You share my earliest memories.

    You never alter.

    I'm here because I know you'll always be behind me.

    If I murdered somebody, you'd hide me.

Sister

    No we wouldn't.

Father

    Betwixt the stirrup and the ground,

    He prayed for mercy, mercy found.

Mother

    Family first.

Everyman

    That's right. Exactly. Family first, Sis.

Mother

    My little boy. Look at you –

    so smart, so prosperous.

    Thank you, son, for making time for us.

Father

    It is the good fortune of many,

    To live distant from the scene of sorrow.

Everyman

    It's just – I have to tell you something,

    incredible and horrible and sick.

Sister

    They don't need any more drama.

    Have you seen the state of your father?

Father

    The door.

Everyman
Dad . . .

Mother
If he's in trouble, we must listen.
It's all right.

Sister
It's not all right!
Let him ask about us
before he starts his 'me myself and I'.
Fair enough, you are my only brother.
But it's yours truly who's stopped here – for years –
caring for our father and our mother.

Mother
You didn't have to.
We could have managed.
She mopes about the place
like collateral damage.

Sister
Don't start, Mother.

Father
The door.

Mother
Face like a sucked lemon.

Sister
Only when I'm emptying your colostomy bag.

Mother
Sir Cliff has one.

Sister
You visit once or twice a year,
breeze in, breeze out.
It isn't good enough.

Everyman
So who paid the bloody mortgage off?

Sister
So who earns the bloody bonuses?

Mother
Twenty-six hours in labour just to give birth to a lesbian.

Father (*starts crying*)
I'm frightened.

Sister
Now look what you've done.

Father
The door.

Mother
How can you cook for a vegan?

Everyman
It's OK, Father, it's OK.
I'm really sorry.

Father
The door. The door.

Mother
Scrambled tofu . . .

Sister
Stop going on about the frigging door!

Mother
Clementine teriyaki . . .

Sister
There's no one at the door.

Everyman
Don't start on Dad!

Mother
Foolishness!

Sister
Twat!

Mother
Five minutes . . .

Everyman
Cow!

Mother
Five minutes in the house and they've started.

Sister
Arsehole!

Everyman
Bitch!

Mother
Stop it, the pair of you!

Everyman
I met Death.

Sister
Name-dropper. Last year it was George Clooney.

Everyman
Death came to me.
Fucking Death!

Mother
My boy, my boy, are you ill?

Everyman
My number's up. I'm so afraid, Mum.
Death stood before me.
It was him! I know it was!
He said I have to take a journey – now –
to God.

You've got to believe me.
I have to give a Reckoning
of what I've done,
how I've spent my Time.

Sister
This is insane.
Are you doing cocaine?
A Reckoning?

Mother
When the Lord is beckoning
at our Time of Reckoning,
the perfect power of prayer will prevail.

Sister
We're not all God-botherers, Mother.

Father
And now . . .

Mother
I have prayed for this family all my life.

Father
– the end is near . . .

Mother
For you,
and you –

Father
– and so I face . . .

Mother
Even for your Father –

Father
– the final . . .

Mother
– standing there like that.

Father
   – the final . . .

Sister
   Curtain.

Mother
   And when I reach God's Holy Kingdom,
   I will carry on praying.

Father
   Curtain.

Sister
   You see what I have to put up with?

Mother
   Don't worry, Son.
   Your mother will be going first.

Everyman
   But I don't want you to go first!
   I want you to come with me.

Sister
   This is off its cake.

Everyman
   Listen, listen. What I thought was –
   what I hoped – is this:
   that you, my . . . kindred . . . would accompany me.
   Support me. Speak up for me.
   You know the best of me.

Sister
   No way. At their age?

Everyman
   But my friends won't do it.

Sister
   Where's Sinead in all this?

Everyman
  We split up. A while back.

Sister
  So we're Plan B, as per?
  Let me get this clear –
  you want the family to stand before God with you?
  Are you for real?

Everyman
  Who else can I take?

Sister
  You can do one, brother.

Everyman
  You're right. I've been an arsehole.
  But help me with this Reckoning.
  I've always seen you all right, haven't I?

Sister
  What about my 'Reckoning'?
  All the things I haven't done yet?
  I've had to be the strong one here
  because you can't cope
  with them getting old and senile and ill.
  You're better than this.

  Door knocks.

Father
  I told you!

Sister
  All right, all right. I'll answer it.

Everyman
  No!

Mother
  Stay where you are.
  You're my son.

I can't stand by and see you in danger.
It's not natural.
Look at him – he's terrified. Come.
Come to your mother's heart. There.
He didn't even like the dentist when he was little.
He used to cry blue murder when you took a plaster off.

Door knocks.

Father
I told you!

Mother
I'll go.

Everyman
Mum! Not you, not you.
I love you. So much.
I love you all.

Door knocks.

Sister
Ev – the back door.
Go that way.

Everyman runs.

Everyman
I hurt and hurt
and Time's a haemorrhage.
My heart. My heart.
It wants to escape from me
before it breaks.
It breaks.
All my mistakes.
What God? What God?
Show yourself!
I don't know you!
You've never answered my prayers.
What about dementia and cancer?

What about my mum and dad?
Cure them.

Who are you?
The creator . . . of the mosquito?
One child dead every thirty seconds
from an insect bite?
Bravo for that, you sick fuck!
If you do exist, you're a wanker.
Answer!
Why should I be judged so soon?
I've done no crime.
I've worked hard, played by the rules.
So bog off with your guilt and your hairshirts.
I'm Somebody! I'm not even ill!
I'll give you a Reckoning:
Money in the bank. An Alfa Romeo.
A fuck-off house with underfloor heating.
Pictures. A signed Tracey Emin.
This Rolex. Is that enough?
Watch this space – 'God'.
I'll buy and buy, take every sign of wealth –
no, more than that, discernment, taste –
to tip your stupid scale.
This plan can't fail!
Bring it on – Worldly Goods!

Goods
We're here, sir, where we always are;
beside the glowing cashpoint where you bow your head,
behind the shopfront window. Come in,
we value you. You value us. He has a loyalty card.
Welcome back
to this cathedral of conspicuous consumption.
All we have is yours to take away.
We can supersize you, sir, upgrade you.
Just tell us what you need from us today.

Everyman

Yeah, you know me, all right.
My consumer profile's in your DNA.
We talk each other's language.
Roll out everything you've got.

Goods

We've got the lot. We aim to please.
Whatever you can pay for, we'll provide.
You see the Royal Warrant on the door?
First floor for perfumes, grooming, jewellery;
and second floor – designer clothes:
Versace. Gucci. Prada. Beckham.
Third floor – Computers. Smartphones. Electronics.
Want more? There's always more.
Fourth floor – investment art, plus private healthcare,
offshore banking, tourism – the Amazon, Africa,
Antarctica, Mount Everest, a cruise to Venice?
Screw the Lagoon – the city is so nice in June.
And then we have floors five and six, exclusive
to our mega-rich. Honours. Knighthoods.
Football clubs. Carbon offset and, of course,
Philanthropy.
Tell us you love us, sir.

Everyman

I do. That's me. For you – true love. Fidelity.
Why not? You sell yourselves as better than sex.
Here's my Visa. Maestro. Mastercard. American
    Express.

Goods

Then whatever in this whole wide world you want
is yours.

Everyman

Run with me on this one.
Hashtag: the customer is always right.

It's not for this world, see, it's for the next.
I have to present myself to God
and give a true account of how I've lived.
Well, this is who I've been –
call it obscene,
but I've always loved my stuff.
I'll take you with me – now –
let's call God's bluff.
No black marks here.
My credit's good.
Got it? Understood?

Goods
It's true, if you are poor in this world, sir,
you're toast. Money talks, it don't keep shtum.
But in the world beyond this – we are dumb.

Everyman
'Sir' thinks otherwise.
I've worked my balls off to possess you on this Earth.
You can prove to God just what I'm worth.
What I'm worth . . .

Goods
Sir, sir, sir, sir, we sing a different song
and we can follow no man to 'beyond'.
We have no heart. Do you think these eyes
have tears? Or that these lips can kiss?
You reckon that these legs can travel anywhere?
Were you to drag us by these wigs
in front of God dot com, you'd stand with zilch.

Everyman
Zilch?

Goods
Nothing.

Everyman
Nothing? Don't tell me you're nothing.

The bottom line:
I prove my grace and style with my Goods.

Goods

But we're no good to you. Yes, while you live,
we're on the credit side. But afterwards?
The debit side. We don't do souls.
We do sales, but definitely not souls.
There's a higher power than us. God's not a fan.
Come on, sir, face facts. Get braver.
By not coming we are doing you a favour.

Everyman

Do what I bloody tell you!
You're bought and paid for!
You're mine!

Goods

You're under the illusion we are . . . thine?

Everyman

Yes!

Goods

No.

Everyman

No?

Goods

No, no, no, no, sir, time to get real.
We're yours to purchase for a while;
a season of benign prosperity,
in which we rust, corrode and basically fuck up
your moral compass. Interest-free.
Small print: we couldn't give a toss for thee.
You men should know
you cannot take us with you when you go.
And when you're dead, another punter stands in line.
So what would help? A snatch of Auld Lang Syne?

Should auld acquaintance be forgot,
and never brocht to mind . . .

Everyman
Bastards! Sons of bitches!
How can God know me
if God cannot see my riches?

Goods
Sir should have thought of this before.
We're closed. Now piss off. Have a nice day.

Everyman
No fucking way!

Everyman throws money.

He arrives at a plastic city in terrible distress.

Have it! Have it! It's useless.
Leave me with 'zilch'.
Nothing. Nada. Nil pointe.
Will that do you?
Blessed are the poor
for theirs is The Kingdom of Heaven.
Is that the deal?
It's worthless, worthless.
What was the point of earning it?
Saving it?
To be humiliated like this?
That's it.
I don't have any other cards
to play, mate.
There's nothing else I can do.
Blessed are the meek
for they shall possess the land –
if that's okay with everybody else.
Blessed are the pisstakers.
Blessed are they that hunger and thirst

for they shall have their fill.
I hunger. I thirst.
Blessed are the merciful
for they shall obtain mercy.
Show me mercy. Show me mercy.
Blessed are those who mourn
for they shall be comforted.
Where's my comfort?
Blessed are the clean of heart
for they shall see God.
I see no God!

What are you looking at? Eh?

Knowledge
You're bleeding looking at me.
Try closing your eyes.

Everyman
I would, but I can still fucking smell you.

Knowledge
Good point, well made.
I stink. But you're afraid.
Have a drink. Take the edge off.
Smirnoff.

Everyman
Thanks.
Thank you.
This wasn't meant to happen to me.
I matter.

Knowledge
I mattered myself once.
As a matter of fact.
Then I fetched up here on the bones of my arse
and everything stopped mattering. Drink it.
I have another bottle here.
I won the Lottery.

Everyman

So did I . . .

Knowledge

Correct.

Welcome to Hell. SE1.

Darkness. Desolation. Shit.

What we want from this world – out of it.

Good health.

Everyman

I'll tell you something about this world.

Nothing lasts.

Fellowship. Kindred. Friends. My family . . .

And possessions are –

Everyman *and* **Knowledge**

– bloody bollocks.

Everyman

All I have, right, is my name

and nothing next to it, but shame, blame . . .

Knowledge

I know.

We're all the same.

Life's just a crying game.

Everyman

I've pissed it up against the wall.

Knowledge

That's the thing with walls.

In my experience, unless you're very tall,

you can't see over them.

You can't climb them.

Everyman

You can't get round them.

Knowledge
  So what you tend to do is this –
  stand back – and piss.

  Kings, Chapter 14, Verse 10:
  Therefore, behold, I will bring evil
  upon the House of Jeroboam,
  and will cut off from Jeroboam
  he that pisseth against the wall.

  It's up here you need it,
  and down there for dancing.

Everyman
  A shithole like this –
  I should have been a better son . . .

Knowledge
  Partner, brother, citizen, colleague, consumer,
    taxpayer, voter, blood donor . . .

Everyman
  I have helped someone.
  I gave a woman a tenner today.

Knowledge
  I recollect.

Everyman
  I could have given her a hundred and never missed it.

Knowledge
  I know where you're coming from.
  Finish it. It's what you need.
  Think of it as a Good Deed.

Everyman
  A good deed.

Knowledge
  Good Deeds . . .

Everyman
Good Deeds.
I need Good Deeds to show to God!

Knowledge
Of course you do, mate.
Dark, though, getting late.

Good Deeds?

Everyman
Good Deeds?

Knowledge
Where else could she be
but in this stinking place?

Everyman
Where are you?
Where are you?

Good Deeds?

God/Good Deeds
Hallelujah, look who it is.

Everyman
You're sick!

God/Good Deeds
That's surprising?
How did you think I'd be?
Fit and able?
No seat for me at your fine table,
but seats for Pride and Gluttony and Lust
and all the rest. Best seats for Goods.

Knowledge
He spits on their names, fair do's.

God/Good Deeds
And then comes crawling back to me?

At this hour?
I wonder why?

Everyman
I'm sorry.
I'm so so sorry . . .

Knowledge
He's well sorry, I can tell.

God/Good Deeds
Bit late for that.
You've put me here, the last place you would ever come
unless you had to.
And I know why you crouch there crying now.
Such fear!
Is Death so near? Don't you have much longer?
What a tragedy that I'm not stronger.

Everyman
My fault!
I've looked away from you too many times.
I didn't give.
But yet, you live!
Will you come with me now?
It's you, if anyone, who can negotiate
and that will count with God.

God/Good Deeds
Negotiate?

Knowledge
He's in a state.

God/Good Deeds
How can I come?
I cannot stand for long.
Don't touch me!
My health was in your hands.
What would I say to your God
in this 'negotiation'?

Knowledge
  Rephrase.

God/Good Deeds
  You thought of the poor.

Knowledge
  Rarely.

God/Good Deeds
  You shared your good fortune.

Knowledge
  Barely.

God/Good Deeds
  You controlled your appetites.

Knowledge
  Scarcely.

God/Good Deeds
  You abused the planet.

Knowledge
  Daily.

Everyman
  So tell me what to do!

God/Good Deeds
  What does it mean to you
  to be a human being?
  Tell me that.
  I'd like to hear it.
  I need to hear it.

Everyman
  I don't know. Help me.

God/Good Deeds
  'Help me, help me!'

Listen to yourself.
What are you made of?
Stardust?
Well, you will be dust again.
Know that.

Everyman
Please.

God/Good Deeds
I can't help you.
I'm broken.
You and all your kind –
You have fractured my faith –
in myself.
I'm so tired.
Go with her.
She'll know your way and will not leave your side.

Knowledge
Like she says, I'll be your guide.

Everyman
To where? To what?

Knowledge
We're out of here. You've pissed on your chips.

Everyman
Why?

God/Good Deeds
Stop whining. Go. Go!

They walk away.

Everyman
No, no, no, no, no.
But I let my Good Deeds leave my house of life
and walk the streets, unnourished, unprotected.
Like that woman.

Why would she stand beside me now
when I did so little?
I've always done so little . . .

Knowledge
Come on. Get a grip.
Rat. Sinking ship.

Everyman
How much time do I have?
I know he's following me.
I smell of fear.
I taste it in my mouth.
Or am I following him?
Where are you taking me?

Knowledge
Oh, shit in a bed.
Come 'ead.

Everyman
Why should I trust you?
I don't know you.

Knowledge
I'm your new best friend, mate, mucker,
feire, pal, buddy, chum, crony, comrade,
course you know me – I'm your familiar.

Everyman
I don't want your voice in my head.

Knowledge
But my voice *is* in your head.
It's the pearl in your oyster.
I'm a fucking poet and I didn't know it.
What's it saying, my voice?

Everyman
Go away!

Knowledge

My voice is your voice.
You say potato, I say potato.
You can't ignore it. No choice.
No choice, chuck.
I quack. I cluck. I blabber. I jabber.
I stutter and mutter. Tune in.
What does my voice utter?

Everyman

I don't need you.

Knowledge

Does it say footprint, legacy, guilty as charged,
up shit creek without a paddle . . .

Everyman

Shut up!

Knowledge

I know some interesting words, me.
Methane. Petroleum. Carbon dioxide.
Neonicotinoid insecticide.

Everyman

My head . . .

Knowledge

Simon says put your hands on your head.
Simon says two degrees warmer. Three degrees warmer.
You and who's army? Tsunami. Tsunami.

*Sings lines from 'Stormy Weather' by Harold Arlen
and Ted Koehler.*

Everyman

My head. My head.
There is a thunder in my head.

*Storm scene. Rubbish swirls around, orchestrated by
Death.*

Weather Reporters
8.9 magnitude earthquake
there will be a tsunami

Religious leaders say
take shelter pray Christian Jewish or Islami

8.9 magnitude we have live film of the tsunami

The waves are up to twenty metres high
What follows may be distressing
Many people die
Up to twenty metres high

Everyman
Forgive me if I didn't save the fucking planet
single-handed.
Sorry. Sorry.

Weather Reporters
Tsunami
Christian Jewish Islami

The earthquake 9.8 on the Richter Scale
Preceded by high gales
Unpredicted

People tearing with bare hands at the rubble

Death toll doubled

The whole area levelled

Death toll trebled

Sea levels rising
Scientists say unsurprising

There will be a tsunami

Everyman
No more! Enough!
I can't look any more!
Stop stop stop stop stop! Desist!

Knowledge
You knew all this.

Storm continues with force. Weather reporters
continue until storm blows out.

Everyman
I kept my head down. Looked away.
There'd always be another day.
The waste.
I thought the Earth was mine to spend,
a coin in space.
I hated the News. The News.
Didn't want to hear it –
floods, fires, melting, burning, droughts, extinctions . . .
too much!
What could I do? Me?
My parents used to watch the News
and then the Weather.
I saw the Weather turn into the fucking News.
I put my hands over my ears,
like a spoiled child. I admit it!
I confess!

Knowledge
Confess to who?

Everyman
To anyone! Everyone!
Who should I confess to?

Knowledge
To him?

Enter Everyboy on scooter.

Everyman
The boy I was.

Knowledge
He had better dreams, that kid.

Everyman
   I see him there . . .
   his Book of Days, brand new, unwritten in,
   pages I'll tear off, leave blank,
   or scribble in the same old words:
   Me, me, me. My needs, my wants.
   But I confess to him
   that I'll look after Number One.
   Say 'not in my backyard'.
   Consume and squander, waste, gratify myself,
   and live his life
   as though it couldn't make a difference to a soul
   or to this Earth.
   I'll fill his bank account. Buy cars.
   Clock up the air-miles on my Frequent Flyer card.
   Take flashy, far-flung holidays,
   get pissed, and tip out all my local currency
   to some poor bastard slaving in Dubai,
   or a mutilated girl, begging in Mumbai.
   I'll let small children weave his carpets
   till they're blind,
   then give two hundred quid to Red Nose Day.
   Lenny Henry will make him cry.
   He'll become a deeply sentimental, shallow guy.

   Top scooter.

Everyboy
   Duh!

Everyman
   I'm just saying.

Everyboy
   It's my birthday present.
   All right? Grandad.

Everyman
   Right. The birthday boy.
   Big day.

Knowledge
Big day.

Everyman
I had one like that once.
From my mum and dad.

Everyboy
Why are you sad?

Everyman
Oh, grown-up stuff.
My life –

Knowledge
He's been a bit selfish.
Give him a go on your scooter.

Everyboy
No!

Knowledge
Go on, show him how to share.

Everyboy
OK – but don't scratch it.

Everyman
Thank you.

Everyboy
You're crying. What have you done?

Everyman
Everything.

Knowledge
Nothing.

Everyboy
You could say sorry.
That might make things better.

Everyman
I'm sorry.

Everyboy
Not to me, stupid.

Everyman laughs.

You're weird.

Everyman
Why's that then?

Everyboy
You've only got one shoe!

Everyman
True.

Everyboy
You're a cry baby!

Everyman
I am.

Everyboy
You've only got one friend!
One shoe one friend one shoe one friend . . .

Knowledge
Ha! One shoe one friend.
A remarkable boy.

Everyman
Remarkable.

Everyboy
Loonies.

Everyman
You're so lucky.

Mother (*from off*)
Everyboy!

Everyboy
I need to go home now.
My sister's making me a cake.

Everyman
Enjoy.

Everyboy
See ya. Wouldn't wanna be ya.

Everyman
Don't eat too much.

Knowledge
And say thank you.

Everyboy
I always say Thank You.

Everyman
You won't.

Exit Everyboy.

He scoots away.
Sorry.
I must show I am sorry.

Knowledge
How do you manage that?

Everyman
Wear rags? Give me your clothes.
Take mine.
They reek. They stink of piss and sweat.
I deserve them.
I should suffer.
Here's my shoe!
Let broken glass slice at my toes.

It hurts. I bleed. That's good, yeah?
More. More hurt. More fucking hurt.

Knowledge
That doesn't necessarily work.
I've tried it myself.

Everyman
No pain, no gain.

Knowledge
It can get seriously out of hand.
You can start to enjoy it.

Everyman
Then I need to pray!
Help me remember a prayer.
The Act of Contrition.
We learned it at school.
Help me remember.

Knowledge
Deus meus, ex toto corde –

Everyman
Sing it! We always had to sing it!

Knowledge
Bastard Latin!
Deus meus, ex toto corde . . .

Everyman
O my God, I am heartily sorry –

Knowledge
– *poenitet me omnium meorum peccatorum . . .*

Everyman
– for having offended Thee,

Knowledge
– *eaque detestor, quia peccando, non solum poenas . . .*

Everyman
   – and I detest all my sins, because

Knowledge
   – *a Te iuste statutas promeritus sum,*

Everyman
   – of Thy just punishments,

Knowledge
   – *sed praesertim quia offendi Te,*

Everyman
   – but most of all because . . .

Knowledge
   – *summum bonum, ac dignum qui super omnia diligaris.*

Everyman
   – I have offended Thee, my God . . .

Knowledge
   Ideo firmiter propono, adiuvante gratia Tua,

Everyman
   – who art all-good and deserving . . .

Knowledge
   – *de cetero me non peccaturum peccandique* . . .

Everyman
   – of all my love.

Knowledge
   – *occasiones proximas fugiturum.*

Everyman
   Who art all good . . .
   And I am all shit!
   No, no, no! Dead language.
   It means nothing.
   It isn't me.

I need to find me!
He was sweet to me.
What else did he say?

Knowledge
Thank you.

Everyman
I always say Thank You, he said.
I always say Thank You.
There must be a better prayer.
Come on – a different prayer!

Knowledge
For the gifts of my body, I give thanks –

Everyman
For the gifts of my body I give thanks –

Knowledge
– at the hour of my death . . .

Everyman
At the hour of my death
For the gifts of my body I give thanks
at the hour of my death.
For the gifts of my body I give thanks
at the hour of my death.
For the gifts of my body I give thanks
at the hour of my death.
And I give thanks for its Strength.
I was grateful for that –

Strength appears.

– my fit, strong body,
getting a sweat on,
feeling the burn.
Good in my skin.
And if I abused it – which I did – I'm sorry.

But I'm grateful for those nights of wine
and feasting,
of buzzes and rushes and highs.

And thank you for my Discretion –

Discretion appears.

– such as it was.
What little thought I gave
to the marvel of now.

For my taste, my tongue, my saliva.

*The Five Senses etc. appear, mirroring Fellowship as in
Prologue.*

I saw the world through these eyes,
Brown eyes, come-to-bed eyes,
eyes bigger than my belly.

I smelled it. This nose. This fine nose.

Touched it. My body in this world.
My strong heart. My ears.

I heard its birdsong and traffic and music,
its human whispers, shouts, laughter, weeping.

Thank you, thank you,
for the sweet, sour, ugly, beautiful, the cool, the crap,
for discord and harmony, rough, smooth,
for the fragrant or foul, the fucking lot of it.
My whole life all I've ever wanted
was to be alive; awaken
to the light and air of here. Now.
Smelling my sweat.
Scratching my balls. Stretching into the moment.
Is it raining? Is it a fine day?

Beauty appears.

My own Beauty in the mirror. My secret vanity.
Or insecurity.

I struggled with them both.
I hold my hand up to it
But teach me the Latin prayer
to give thanks for my sensuality,
my sex drive, my passion.
But my dread of commitment.
My ducking and diving,
my skiving, my evasions . . . my credible lies
to Catherine.
Ayesha. Emma . . .
William.
Helen. Sinead.
Sinead . . . my conscience.
I have been a loving man
who has hurt people
and been hurt. Yet been so loved.
But I admit my fear, my boredom . . .
my parents sitting in their chairs for years . . .
Not for me. No way.
Same neighbours. Same holiday.
Not good enough for my arrogance.
That's who I am. I know it.
Thank you for my Knowledge:
that I'm restless.
Ambitious. Bloody-minded.
Stubborn – even now.
Even now, egotistical;
wanting to be liked,
to come out on top, to win,
to close the deal.
I own such pointless obsessions –
my work ethic,
my ability to pitch,
my stupid competitiveness.

My wheeling and dealing.
All of it – bad and good
that make me human on this Earth.
How else can I know myself?
For my kindness, *deo gratias*.
For my loyalty.
But I have been a thoughtless bastard.
A Jack-the-Lad. A smooth operator.
A laugh. A dude. A hypocrite.
A ragbag of a man,
made up of you, and you,
of all of you.

The Senses etc. join in.

I have followed Lust instead of Love.
I have envied my peers.
I have wallowed in Sloth, in Greed, in Gluttony.
I have let my Anger off its leash,
and let Pride govern every inch of me.
I should have praised my eyes – for Venice,
the paintings of Turner, Picasso, Van Gogh,
a man on the moon, Lionel Messi.
One holiday in Blackpool as a boy
I saw elephants walking on the beach.
Every morning after that, my mum
took me down to see the elephants.
This will kill my mother.
My beautiful mother. My beautiful mother,
who fought for me every inch of my childhood.
Who stayed with my father all those years
just to keep the family together.
My father, whom I never really understood –
with his discipline,
and his fucking rule book,
and his 'My Way or the Highway'.
So I just walked away

and left my sister to deal with it.
And never thanked her.
Never thanked any of them. Any of them.
Thank you.
Praise to my ears for my mother singing,
for Mozart, Bach,
the Beatles, Michael Jackson,
church bells, the blackbird's song,
the mad joy of a school playground,
wind in the trees, like an ocean of air.
Praise to my nose for wet dogs, hyacinths,
my father cutting the grass outside my window,
Sinead's scent on my pillow.
Petrol – filling up my car.
Christmas – someone smoking a cigar.
Praise to my tongue for snowflakes, tequila,
marzipan, mint, cheese and honey, every kiss.
Every kiss.

Praise to my hands, these sweaty, trembling hands,
these gentle hands,
these fists of hands, these grasping hands,
hands which caress, applaud, take, make, break . . .
Give me your hands.

Strength, Discretion, Knowledge, Beauty *and* **Senses**
(*clamouring to celebrate*)

The brilliant luck of it –
To have been here at all!
We did go to the fucking ball.
Swam bollock-naked in the sea
with our mates.

That first time we saw Sinead.
It was like even the air around her
was beautiful.

Top moment – thirty-one.
Scuba-diving in the coral reef.
Absolutely beyond belief.

No, no, no – the best bit, right,
Was losing our virginity.
Sixteen. Philomena McGear
Down at Dad's allotment
We think of it every time we smell parsnips.

Fish and chips on the North Pier
with our dad.

Bumping into the mirror in our mum's bedroom
and not knowing it was us.

Crying. Crying in our cot.
We didn't even know our name.
And then she came.

All

*Lift up your hearts Emmanuel's friends
and taste the pleasure spirit sends,
Let nothing cause you to delay,
but hasten on the good old way.*

*For I have a sweet hope of glory in my soul
For I have a sweet hope of glory in my soul
For I know I have, and I feel I have,
A sweet hope of glory in my soul.*

*Though death may now his powers employ
Our happiness for to destroy
Yet never fear, we'll gain the day
By marching in the good old way*

*For I have a sweet hope of glory in my soul
For I have a sweet hope of glory in my soul
For I know I have, and I feel I have,
A sweet hope of glory in my soul.*

For I have a sweet hope of glory in my soul
For I have a sweet hope of glory in my soul
For I know I have, and I feel I have,
A sweet hope of glory in my soul.

Everyman

Aged forty. I got wrecked at my birthday party
and I fell off the roof.

There is more.
There is more in me.
The blossom on that tree.

God/Good Deeds

The moon rises.
It shines on your grave.

Everyman

The lovely, empty moon.
Time to be brave.

God/Good Deeds

Or rage. Or cry.
There are many ways to die.

Everyman

What's my way?

God/Good Deeds

I would say –
you're taking it very personally.
I hate to admit it,
but I'm touched. Truly, I am.

Everyman

But why?

God/Good Deeds

All this – the tree, the setting sun,
the moon, each blade of grass, the Earth,

your place in it – oh, you're warm, you're warm –
your love, your useless, feeble guilt . . .
I see it matters to you.

Everyman
Every moment.

God/Good Deeds
Bless you.

Death
Aww – 'every moment'.
I love it – all this claptrap.
Job satisfaction doesn't cover it.
It's more . . . a joy.

You missed yourselves at the Fall of Troy.
And as for the mortal panic
on the *Titanic* –
The musicians scraping away
at 'Those in peril on the sea'?
Meat and drink to me.
And I was there, of course, doing overtime,
for each execution in the French Revolution.
Happy days. The guillotine. The audience.
The look on Robespierre's face!
But, see now, when the head fell off
into the basket,
he looked around for a while,
and I'm telling you
                    he was literally clocking where he was.
Stop me now – or I'll be here all night
with this stuff.
                    So – only a moment
since I slipped *him* the bad news
and yet his head knew everything
in those few seconds.
What's the time, Mr Wolf?

Knowledge
  We know what time it is.

Death
  You – smart arse – button it.

  Death begins to corral them.

Strength
  Get out of here. Back off.

Death
  Not so strong now, eh?
  Come on then, if you're hard enough.
  Not so clear-sighted now?
  Not so sharp-eared?
  Do you smell a rat?
  What's that taste in your mouth?
  Is it bile? Is it vomit?
  Am I freezing to touch?

Beauty
  My hair! My teeth!

Death
  You look like death.

Strength
  What's happening?

Death
  Use your discretion.

Strength
  Tell us!

Everyman
  I HAVE TO DIE!

Beauty
  I'll decompose! I'll rot!
  Be food for worms!

Don't take me!
You can't make me!

Everyman

You cannot live without me!
None of you.
You die with me.
Are you stronger than death?
Are you cleverer?
Can't you see? There?
That is my grave.

Sight

Not into the dark.
I won't go into the dark.

Everyman

You have no choice.

Sound

Nooo . . .

Death

Get over yourself.
Time for my favourite bit of the whole
kit and caboodle.
The last words.
Wait till you hear this.

Senses *and* **Qualities** (*uttering the last words*)

I don't want anyone to see me like this.
No one's to look at me.
Not in this state.

Take my sperm.
She wanted my baby.
Get some sperm out and freeze it.
Tell her.

Rollo! Here boy! Here boy!
Good dog. Come on! (*Whistles.*) Here boy!

I want to go home. 37 Beltane Street.
37 Beltane Street. 37 Beltane Street.

I went out to the hazel wood,
Because a fire was in my head . . .

Is that it then?
What was the fucking point?

. . . And cut and peeled a hazel wand,
And hooked a berry to a thread . . .

There's something I have to tell you.
It's difficult. It'll be hard to hear.

. . . And when white moths were on the wing,
And moth-like stars were flickering out . . .

(*Sings.*)
I feel love . . .

. . . I dropped the berry in a stream,
And caught a little silver trout.
When I had laid it on the floor
I went to blow the fire a-flame . . .

Mama.

. . . But something rustled on the floor,
And someone called me by my name.

Kiss my arse.

Grobbelaar . . .

What time is it?
Why is it dark?
Open the curtains.

. . . Nicol . . .

It was all my fault.

All down to my pride.
But I loved you. You were perfect.

. . . Hansen . . .

Mam.

. . . Lawrenson. Kennedy. Barnes. Molby. Whelan.
Houghton. Rush. Dalglish.

Mam.

*All sing lines from 'You'll Never Walk Alone' by
Rodgers and Hammerstein.*

Mam.

Birthday Rap.

Don't cremate me.
I don't want to burn.

I need you to leave.
I can't die with someone watching me.

As I lay down my head to sleep.
As I lay down my head to sleep.
As I lay down my head to sleep.

Tell my sister.
I want my sister here.

Kiss my arse.

Don't cry. Don't cry.
Look after yourself.

I am still alive!

Put the light on.
I don't want to do this in the dark.

Kiss my arse.

We should have had a child.
You wanted a baby.

Tell them I said something important.

Kiss my arse.

End of Rap.

Happy fucking birthday.

By the end of the last words Death has claimed the Senses and Qualities.

Everyman
I think I have a soul.
In all humility, I think
I have a soul.
Where will it go?
To Nothingness?
When I was a child,
I'd lie in bed in the dark,
eyes tight shut,
and hold my breath –
just to imagine death.
But then a car
would sweep its headlights round my room
and end the game.

I think I have a soul.
Will it go to God?
God, if you are everywhere,
you were too difficult to comprehend
for one, weak, human man.
Forgive me that,
if you exist, allow my doubt.
But if I managed one good thing,
then count that in.

I think I have a soul –
like this planet has a moon –
my own soft light,
when there is only endless night.
Let it go free of Time,

of days and years and death,
of hope and memory.
In all humility,
let it go free of me –
I think I have a soul.

Death

What's this?
'Forgive me, I could have been betterer'?
Et-fucking-cetera.
Hath they all forsaken Thee?
My Boss is ready for a word.
What I suggest
is roll into that clammy pit
and have a nice long kip.
My work is done,
but let me tell you, son,
I've loved the hunt.

Everyman

Can I tell you something?
You're a cunt.

God/Good Deeds

Enough. He is already dead.
His parents weep beside his stone
with wilting flowers.
His friends are singing at his wake.
His sister packs his Goods into a box.
Another man's promoted to his job.
The lawyers have his Will.

Death

Thy Will be done.

God/Good Deeds

It will indeed.
I see his soul, its flickering little flame.
I am well pleased.

Religion is a man-made thing.
It too will pass.
It rains.
The soil will grow new grass upon this grave
in time.
And as for Time, it's time
to bring him for his Reckoning with me.
I love this man –
and I, to every man, must give
perpetual love.
It cannot die. My tragedy. Absurd.
But there we are –
in the Beginning was the Word –
one way of putting it.
Let there be light
and let him see his God.

Exit God/Good Deeds and Everyman.

Death
Help me out here –
did my feckin ears deceive me
or did your man call me a cunt?
This is a total affront.
Where's the respect?
I'm to pick up my scythe
and exit stage left?
I don't think so.
No, no, no, not at all.
See now,
I'm at my most unpredictable
when I'm vexed.
Eenie meenie miney mo . . .
Who's next?

End.